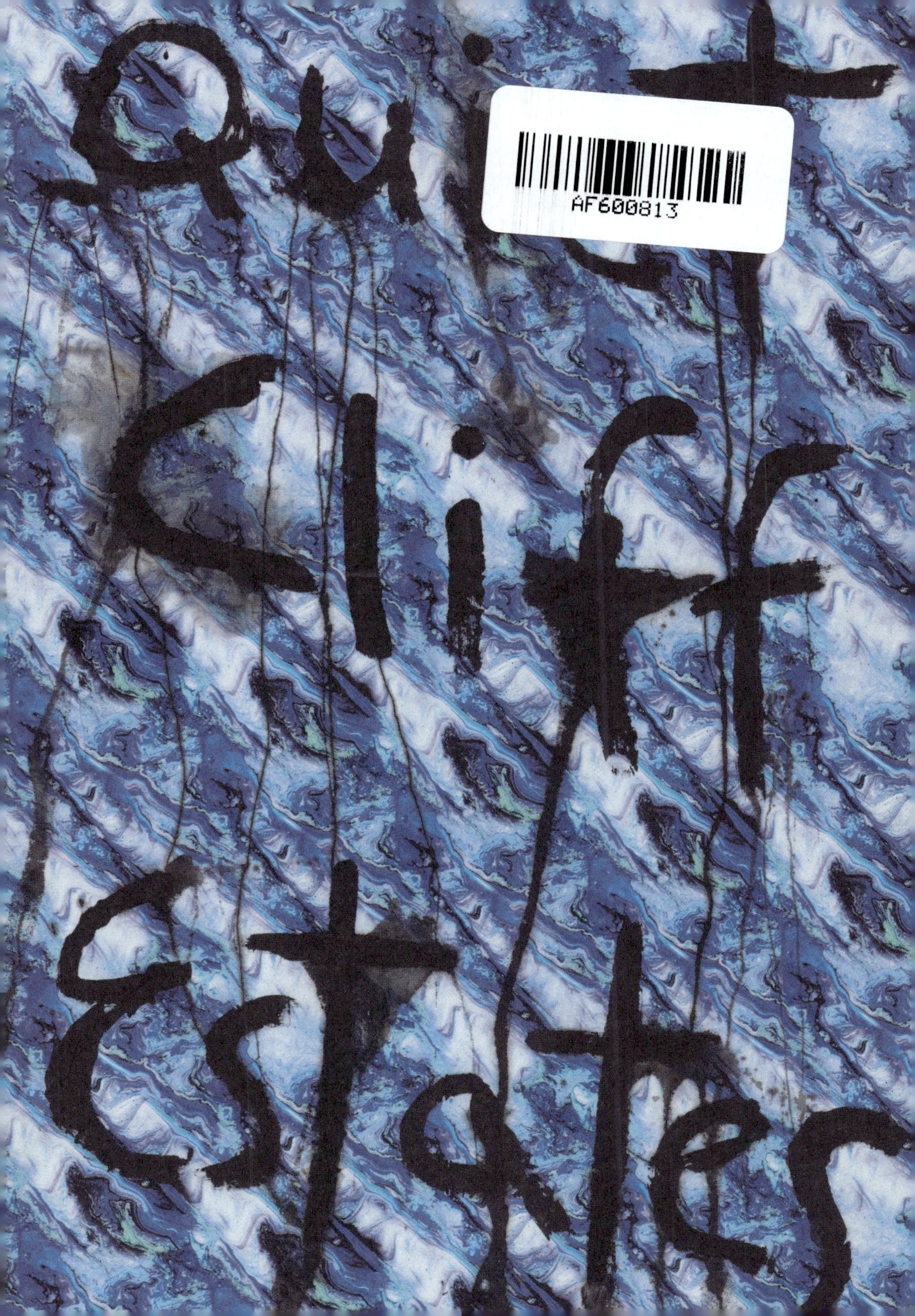
Cliff
estates

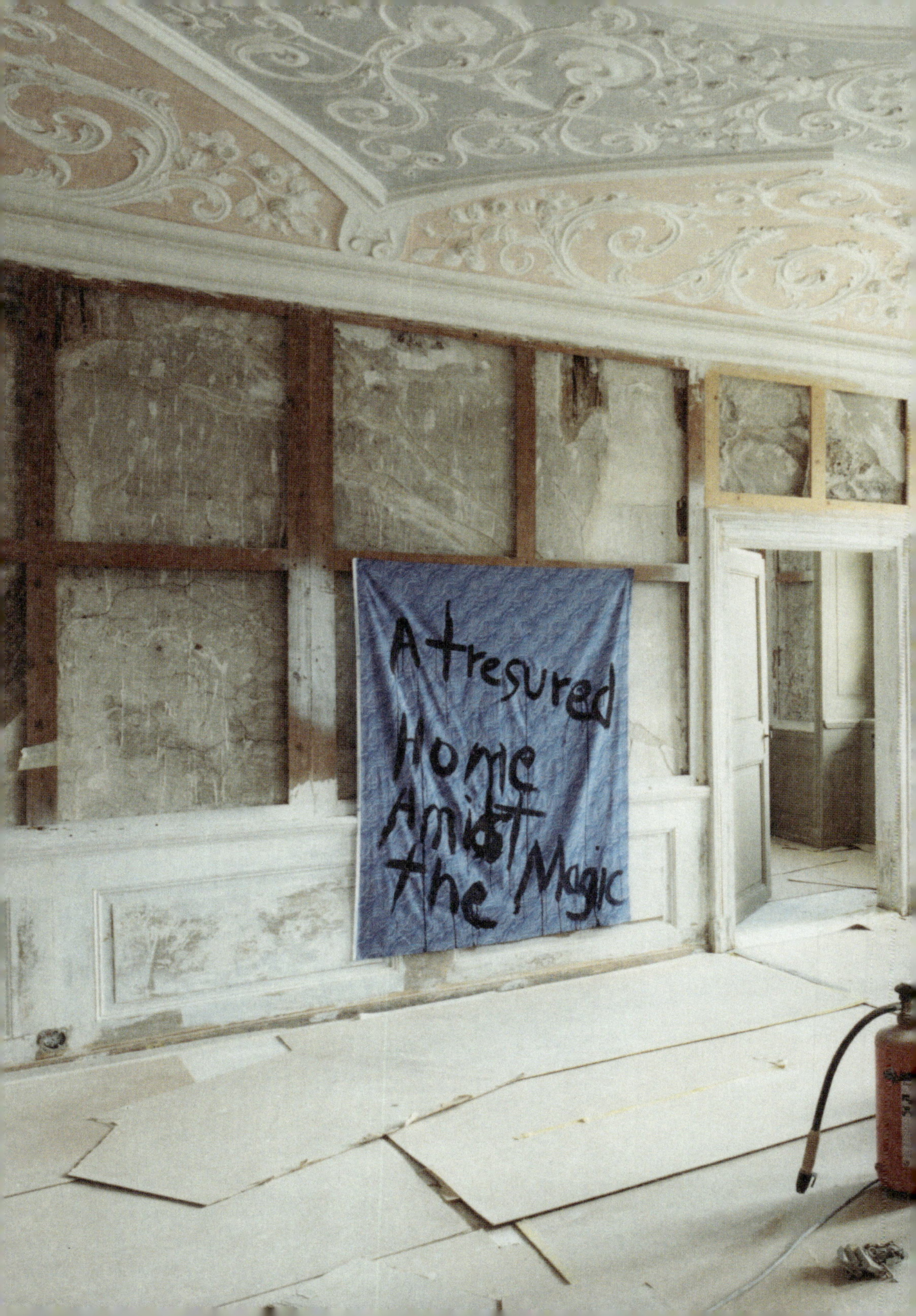
A tresured
Home
Amidst
the Magic

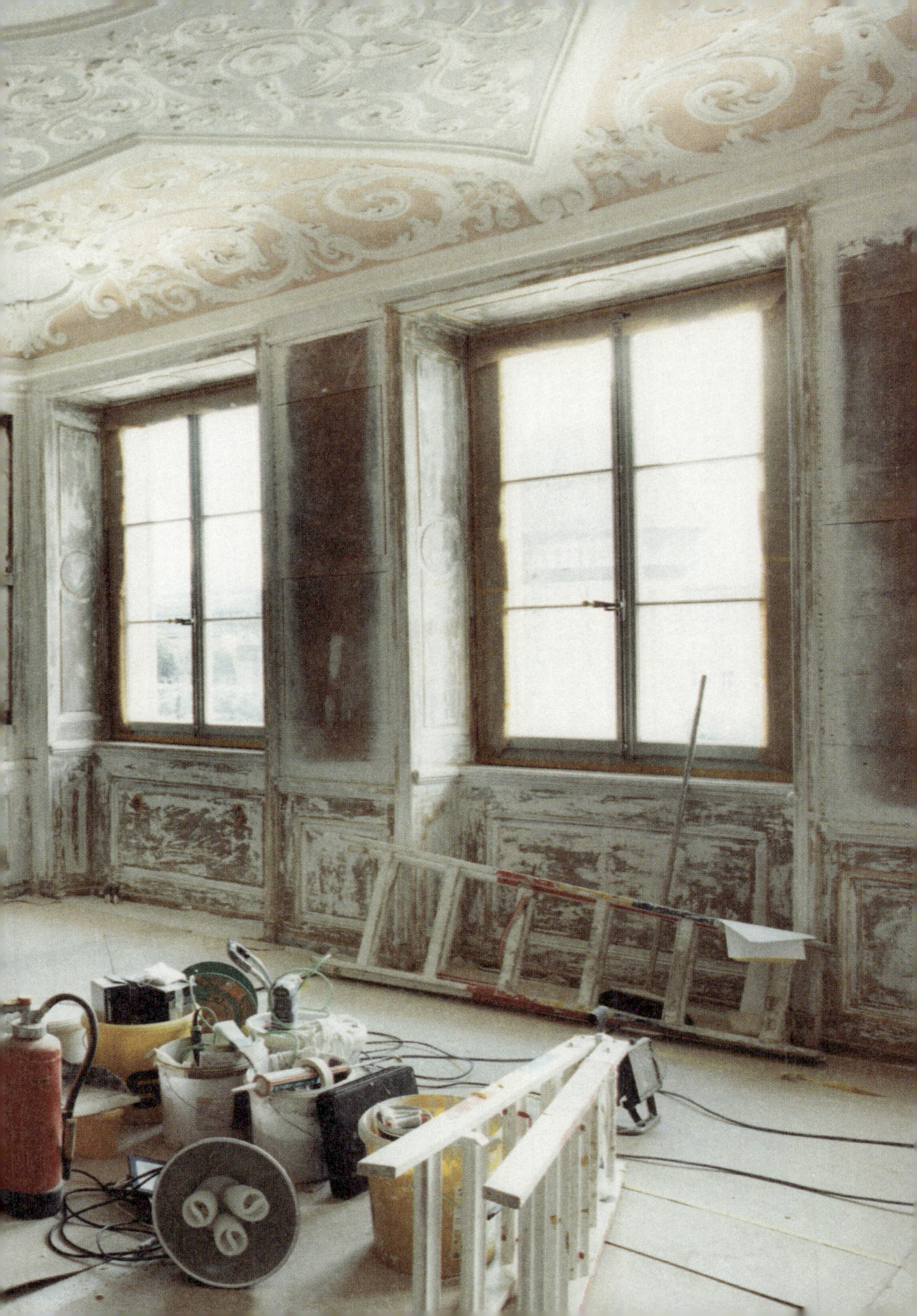

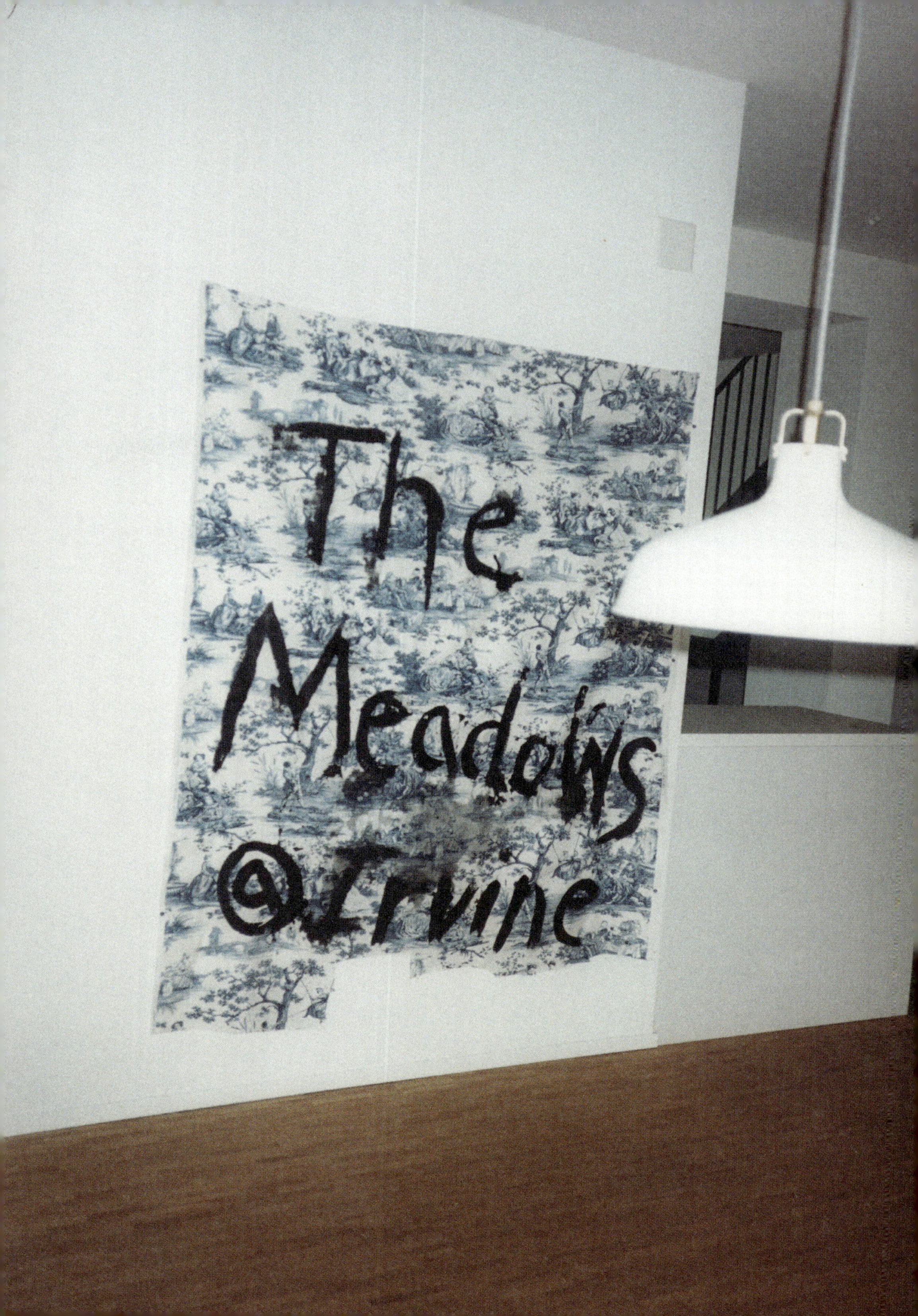
The
Meadows
@Irvine

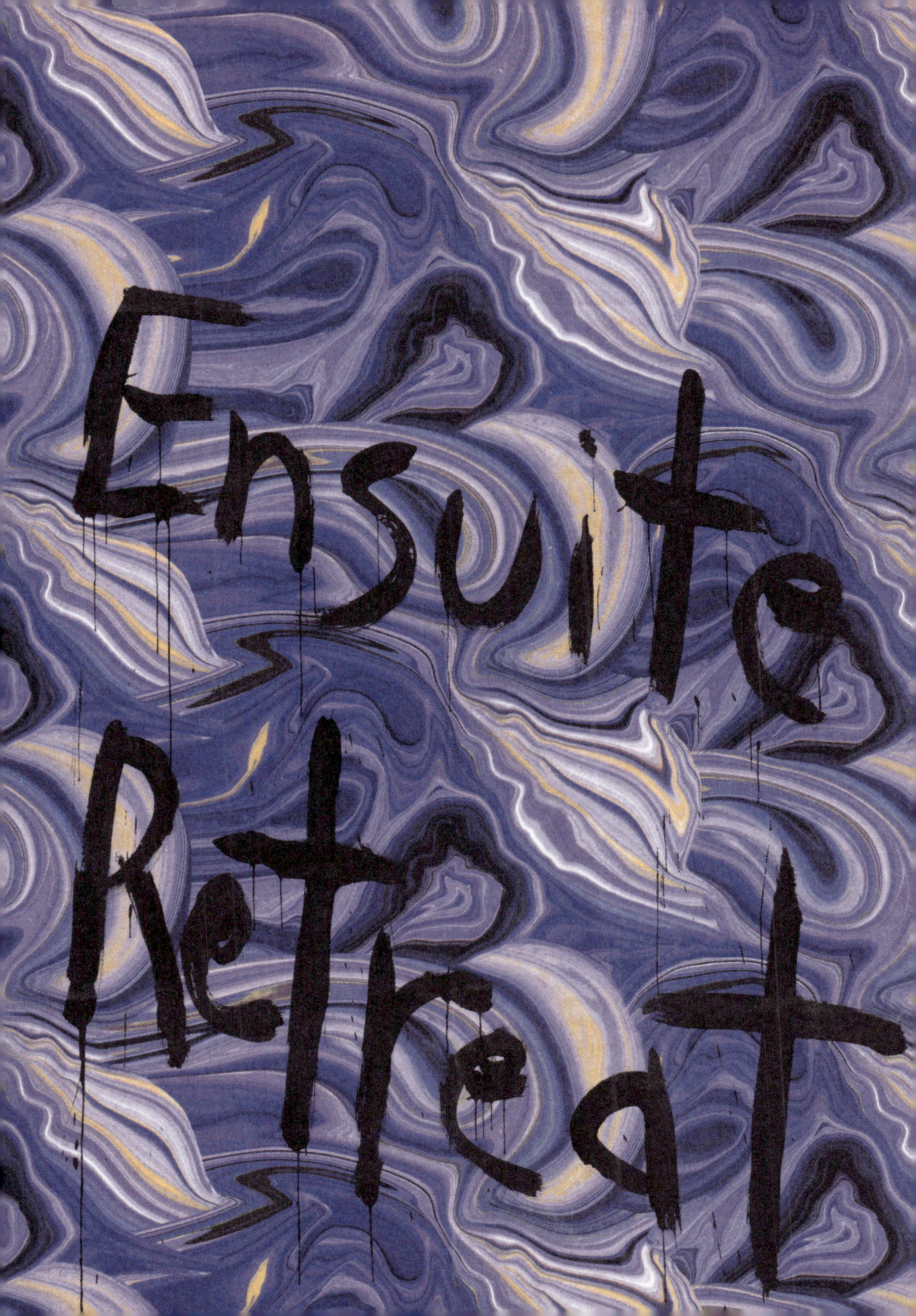
Ensuite
Retreat

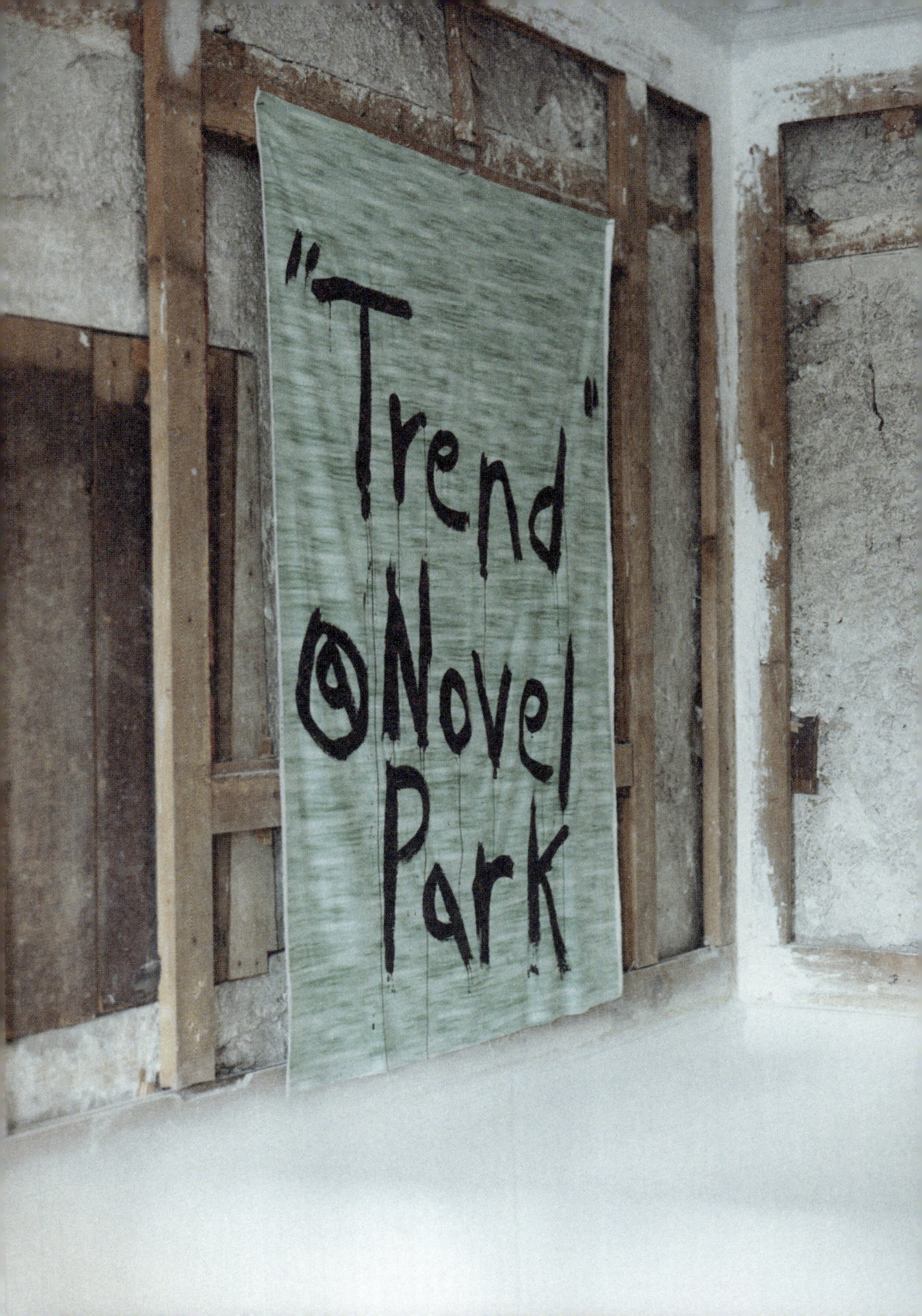
"Trend"
@Novel
Park

Serenity
Security
Private
Paradise

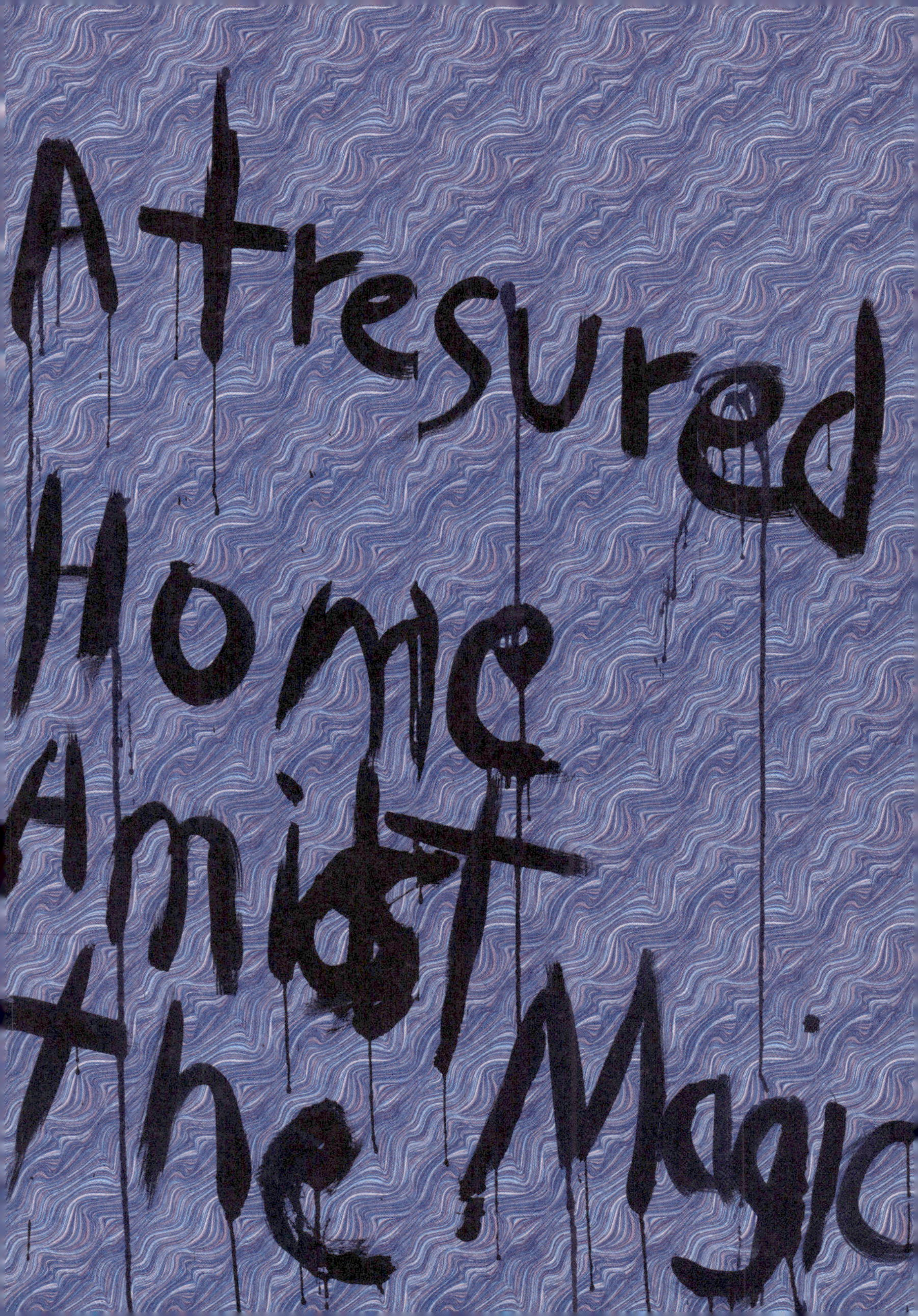
A tresured
Home
Amist
the Magic

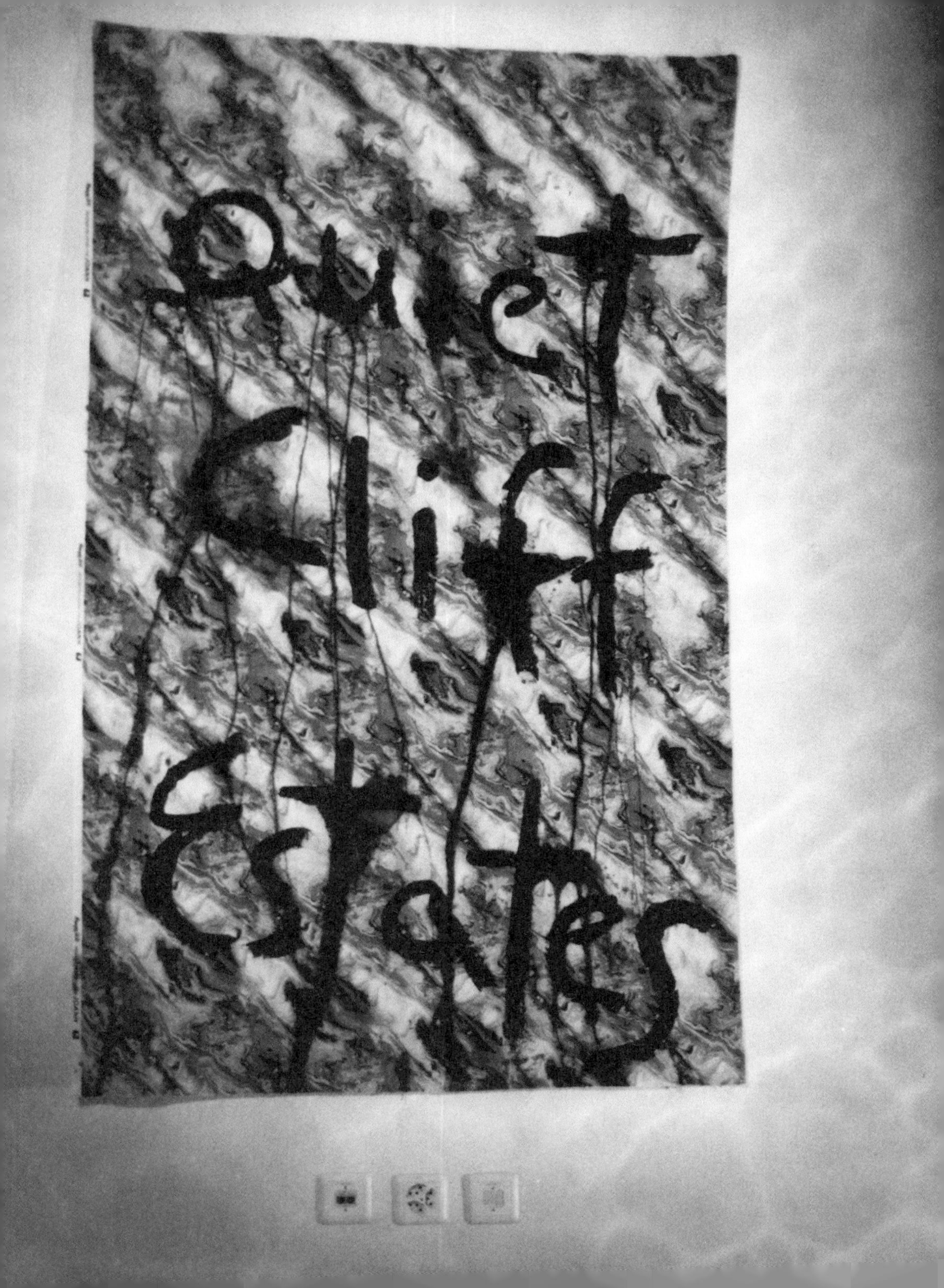

Quiet
Cliff
Estates

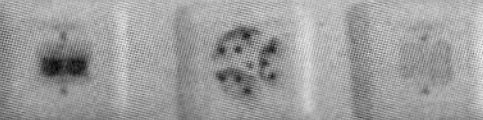

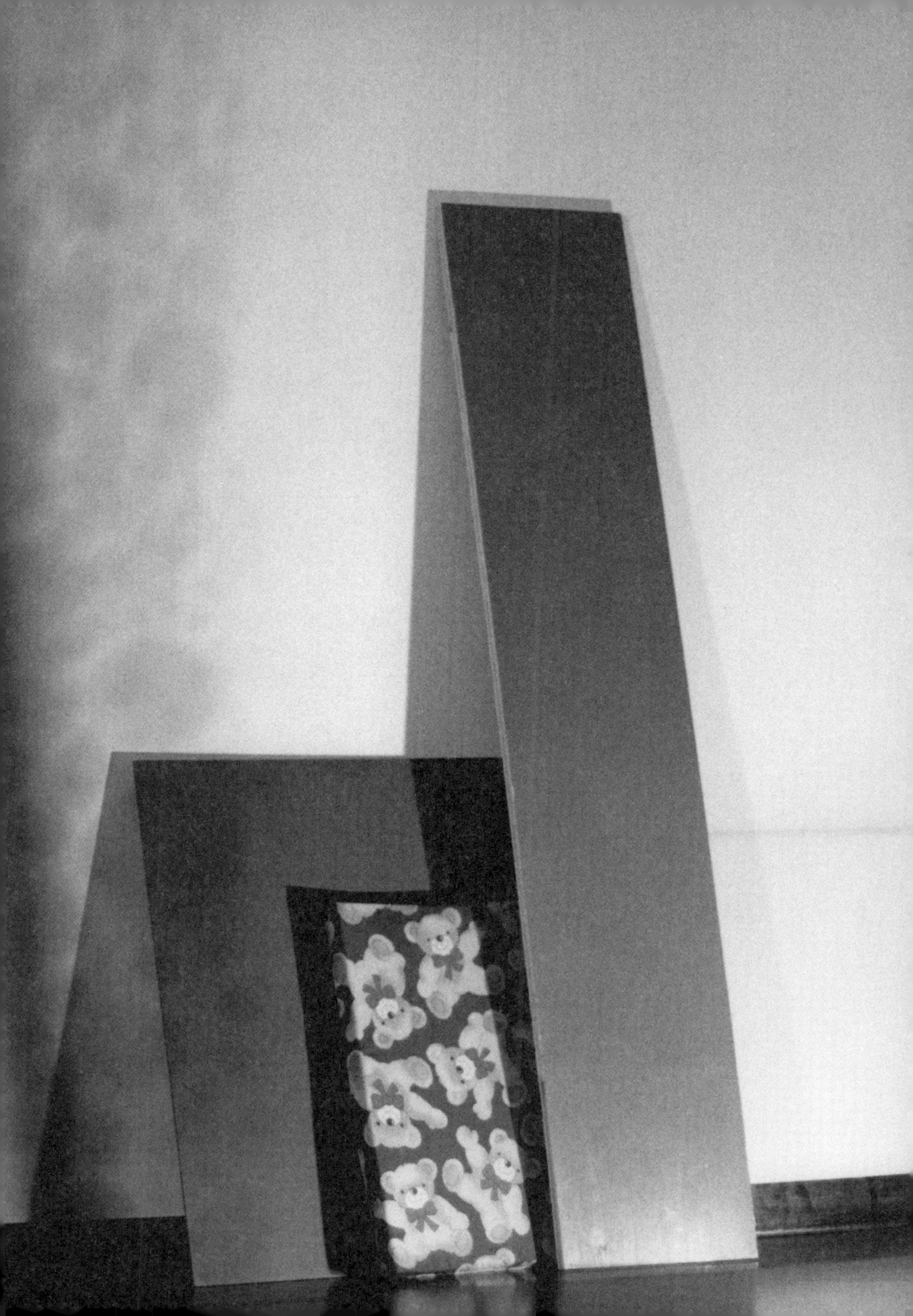

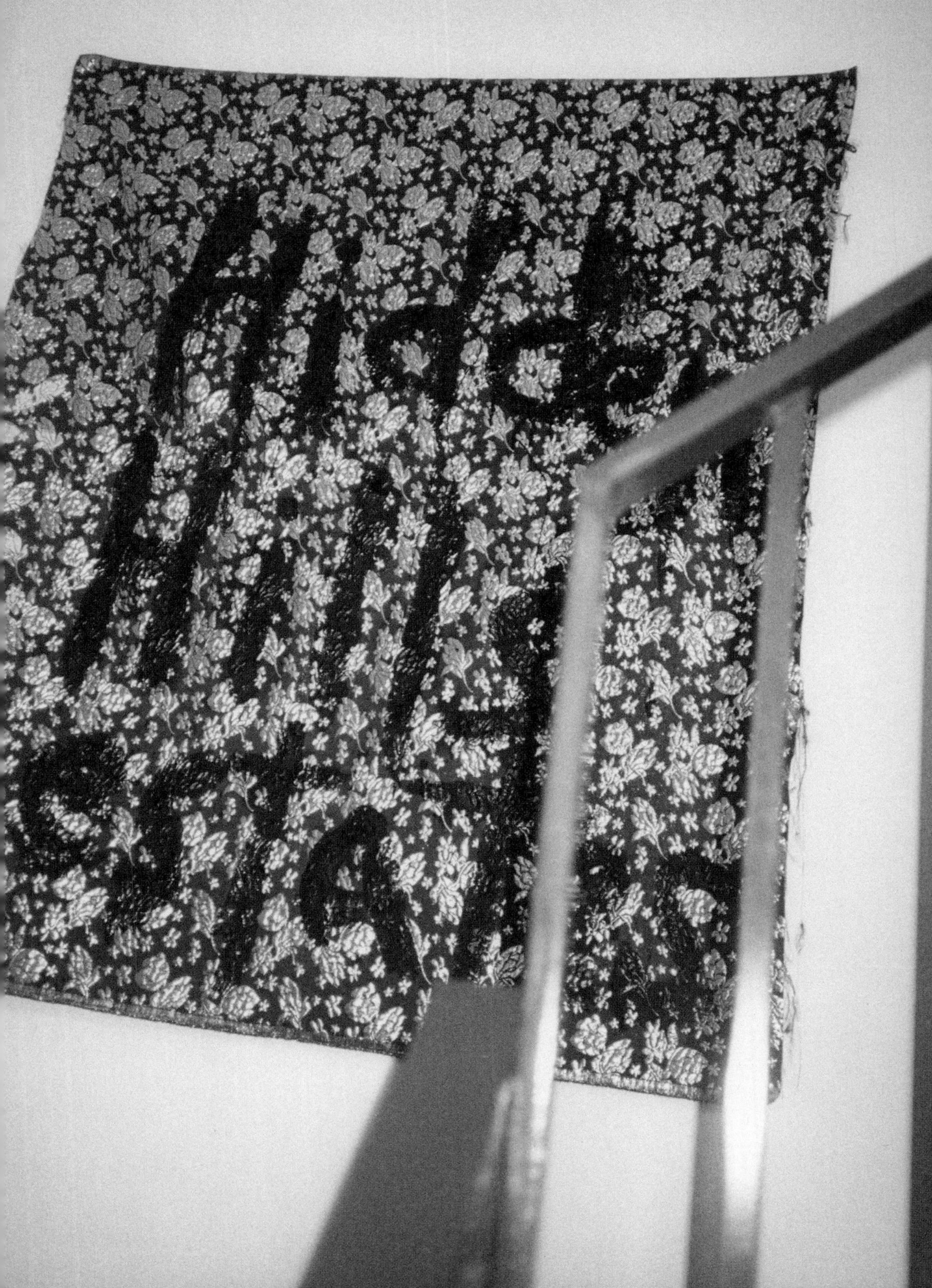

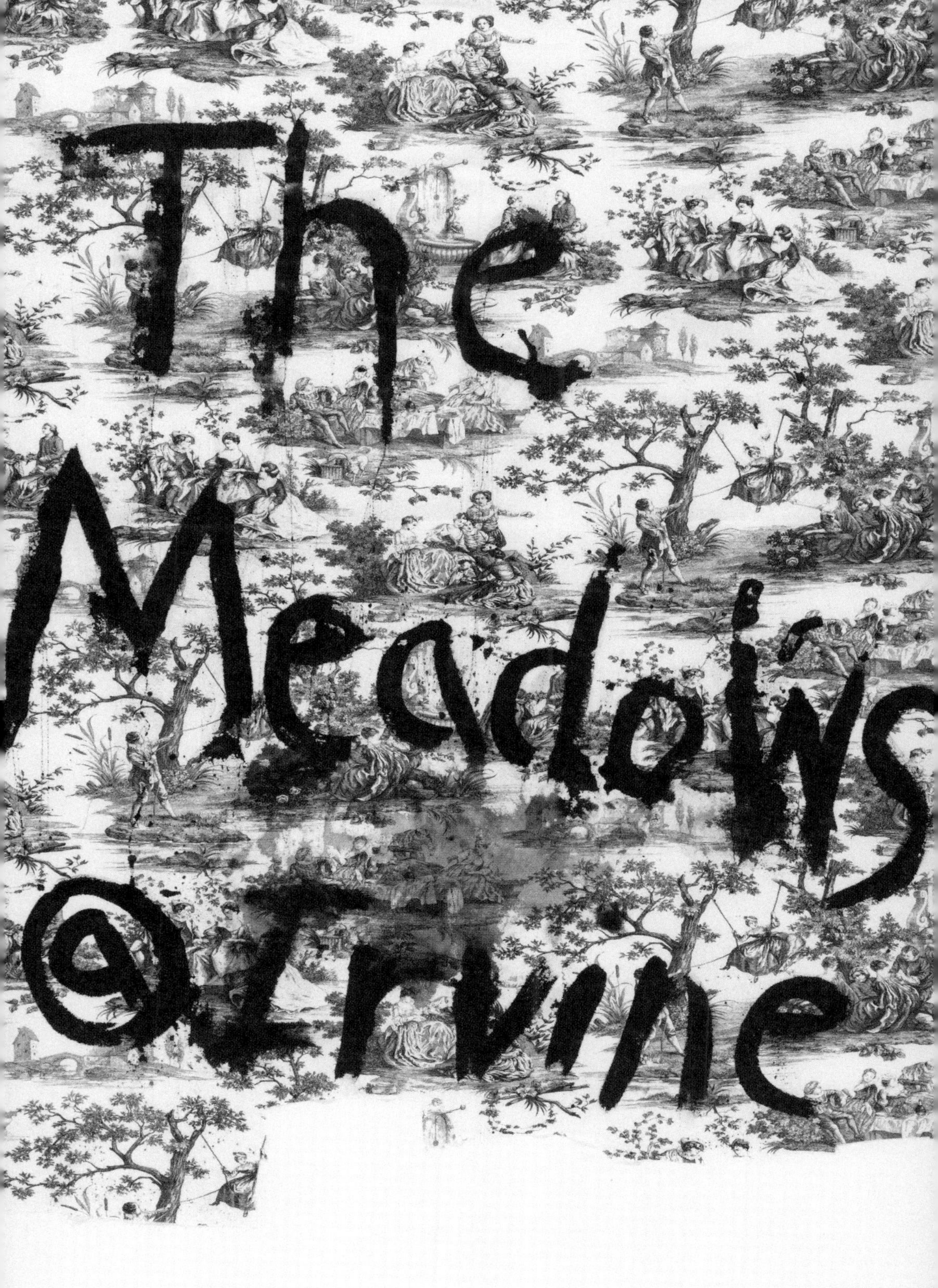
The
Meadows
@Irvine

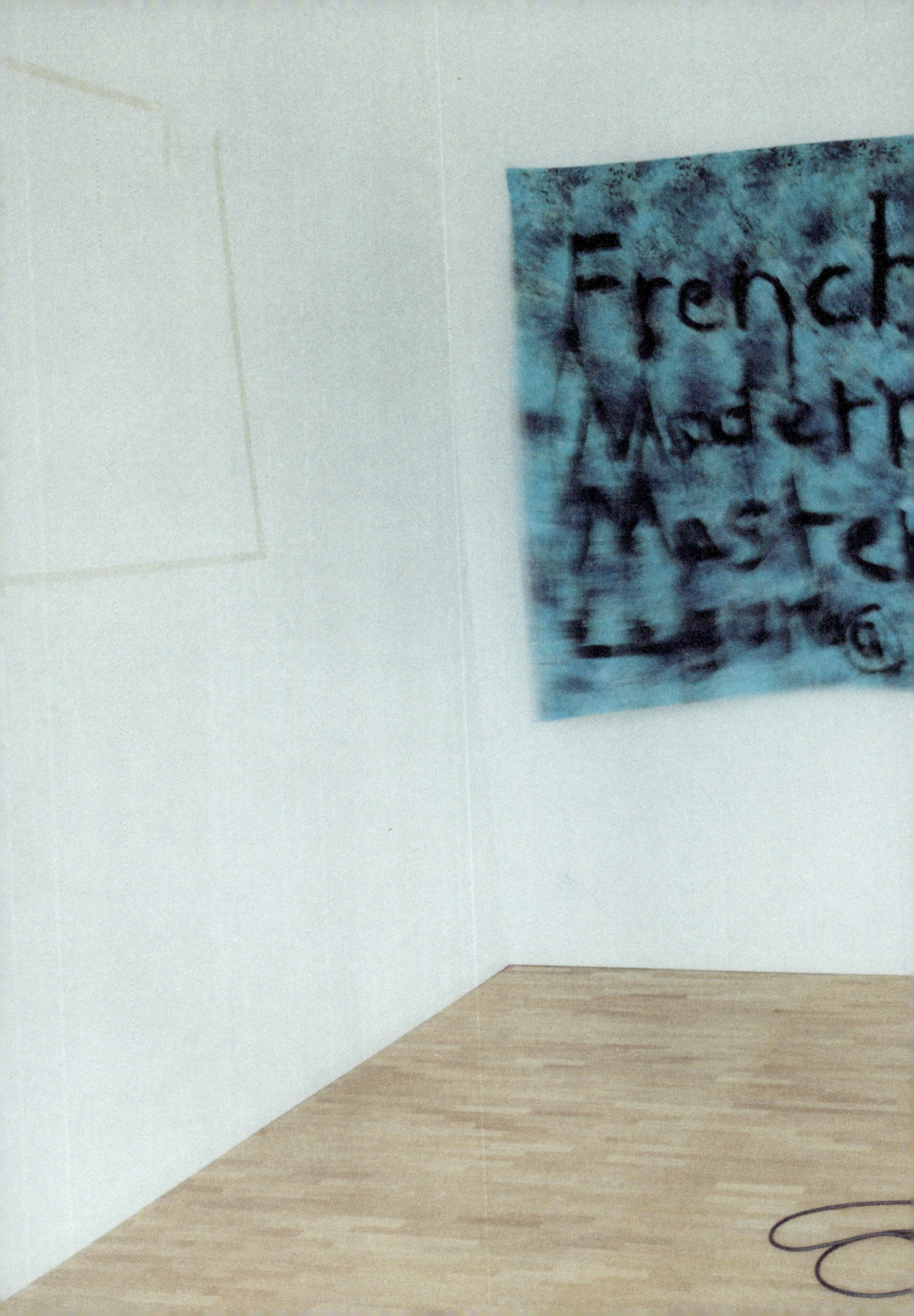
French

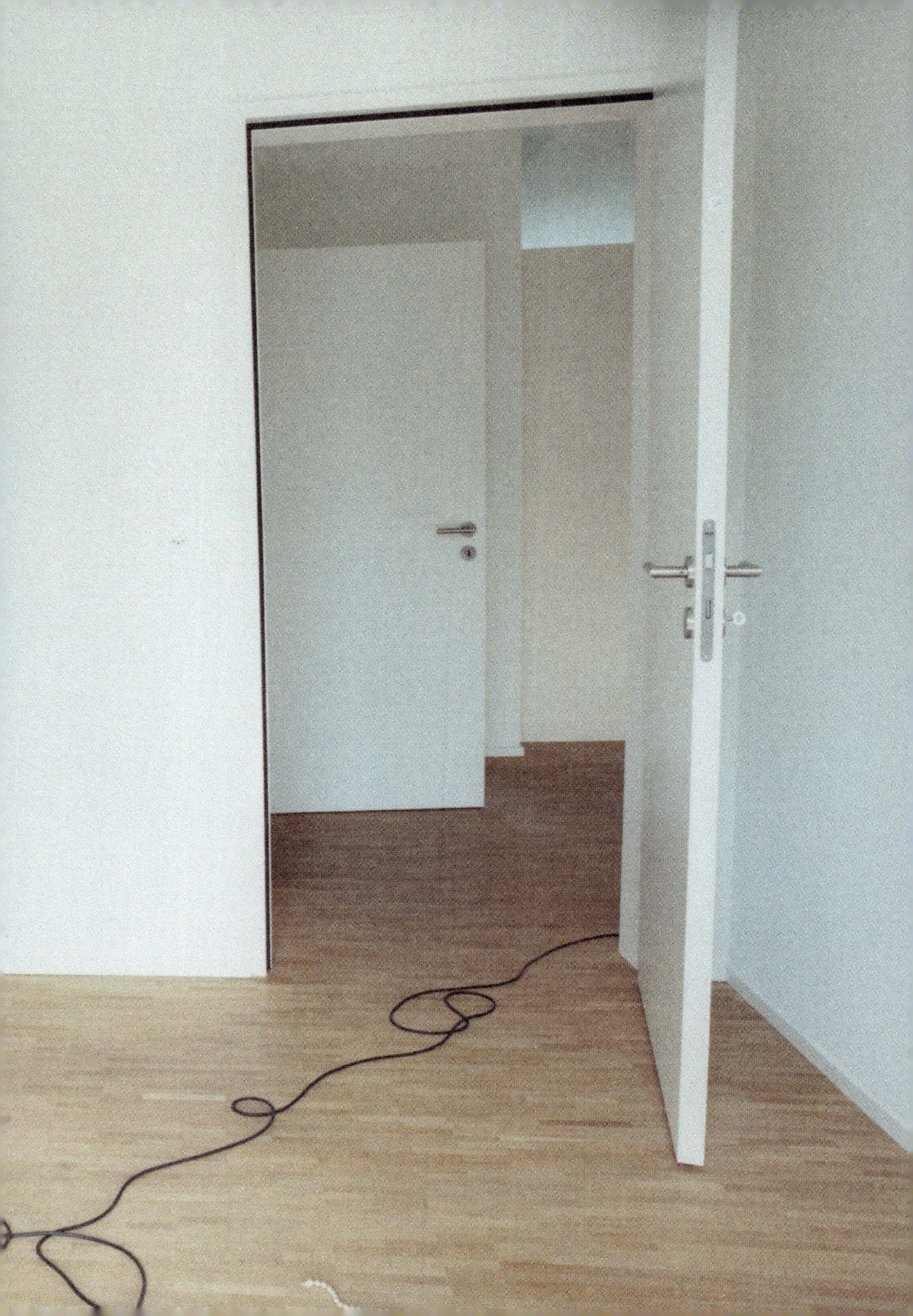

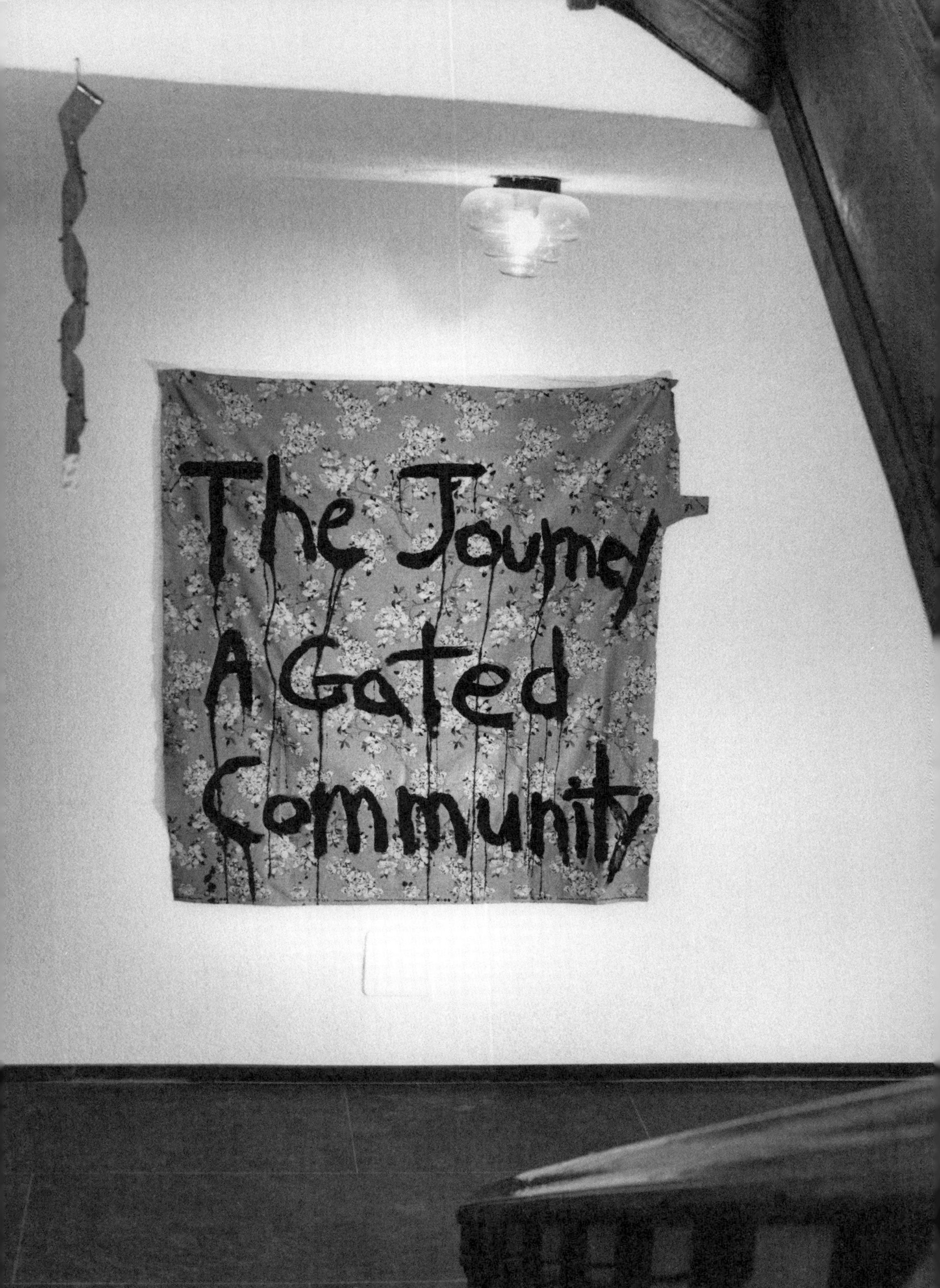
The Journey
A Gated
Community

Hidden
Valley
collection

Loping
Hills
Estates

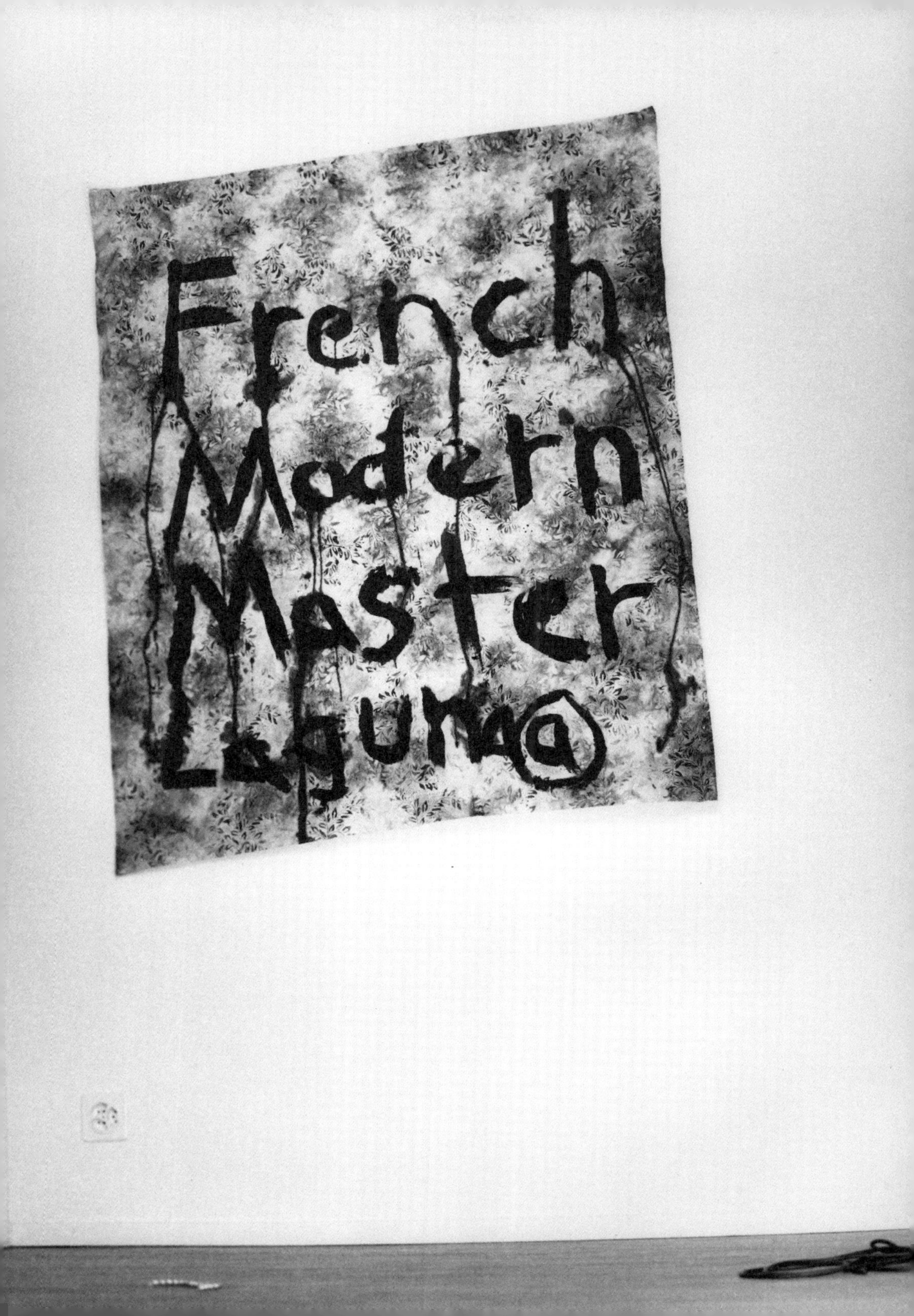

French
Modern
Master
Laguna@

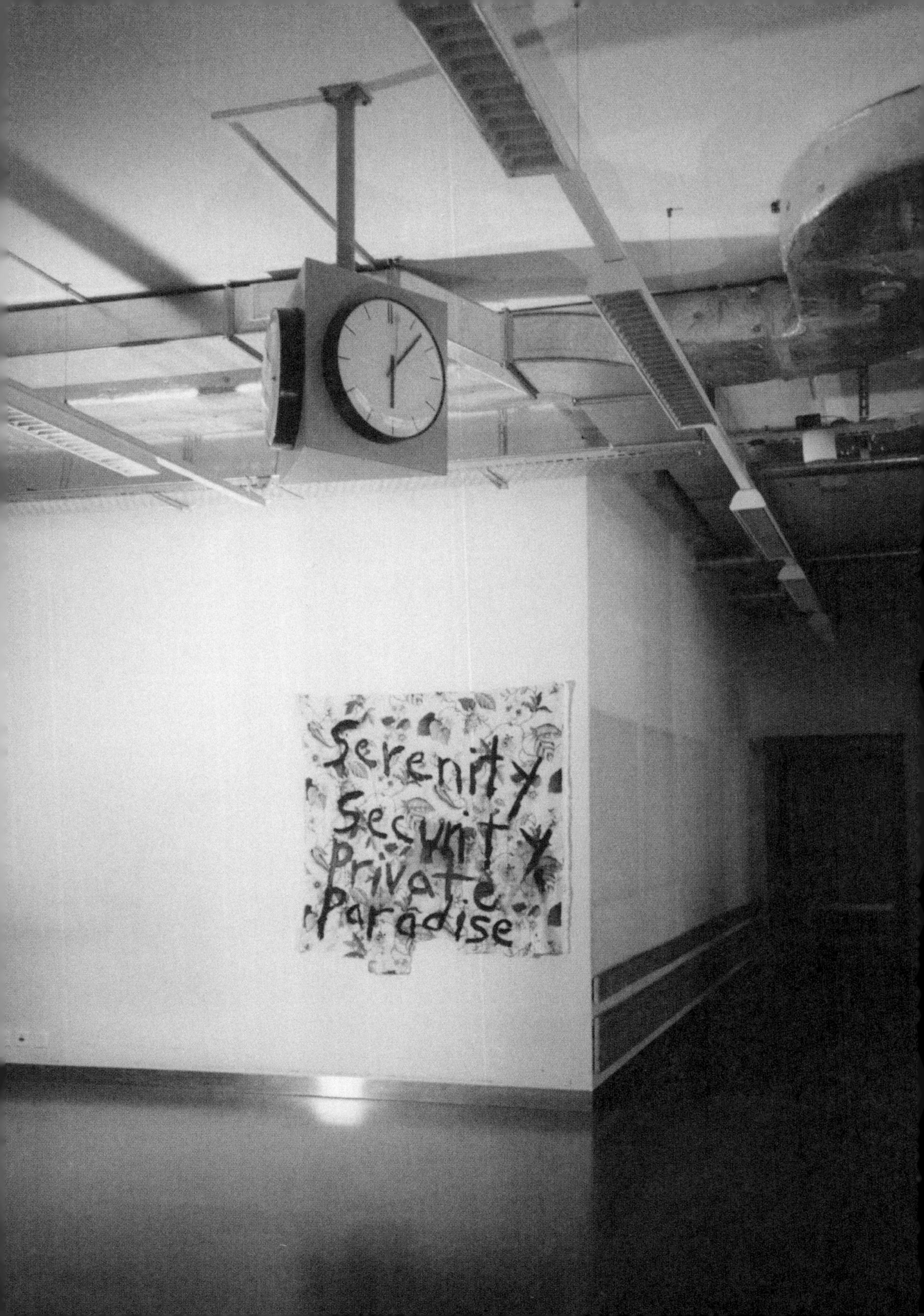
Serenity
Security
Private
Paradise

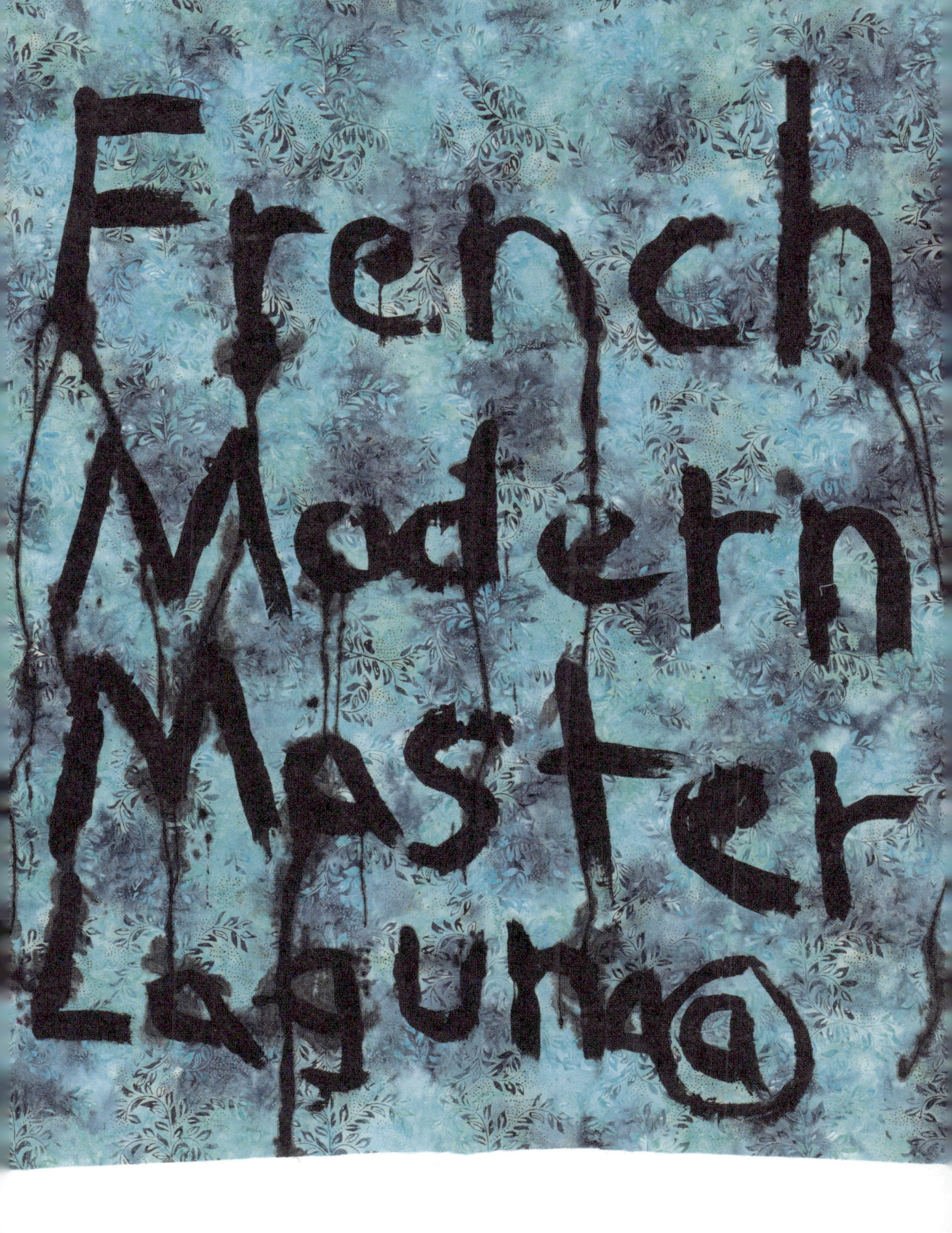
French
Modern
Master
Laguna

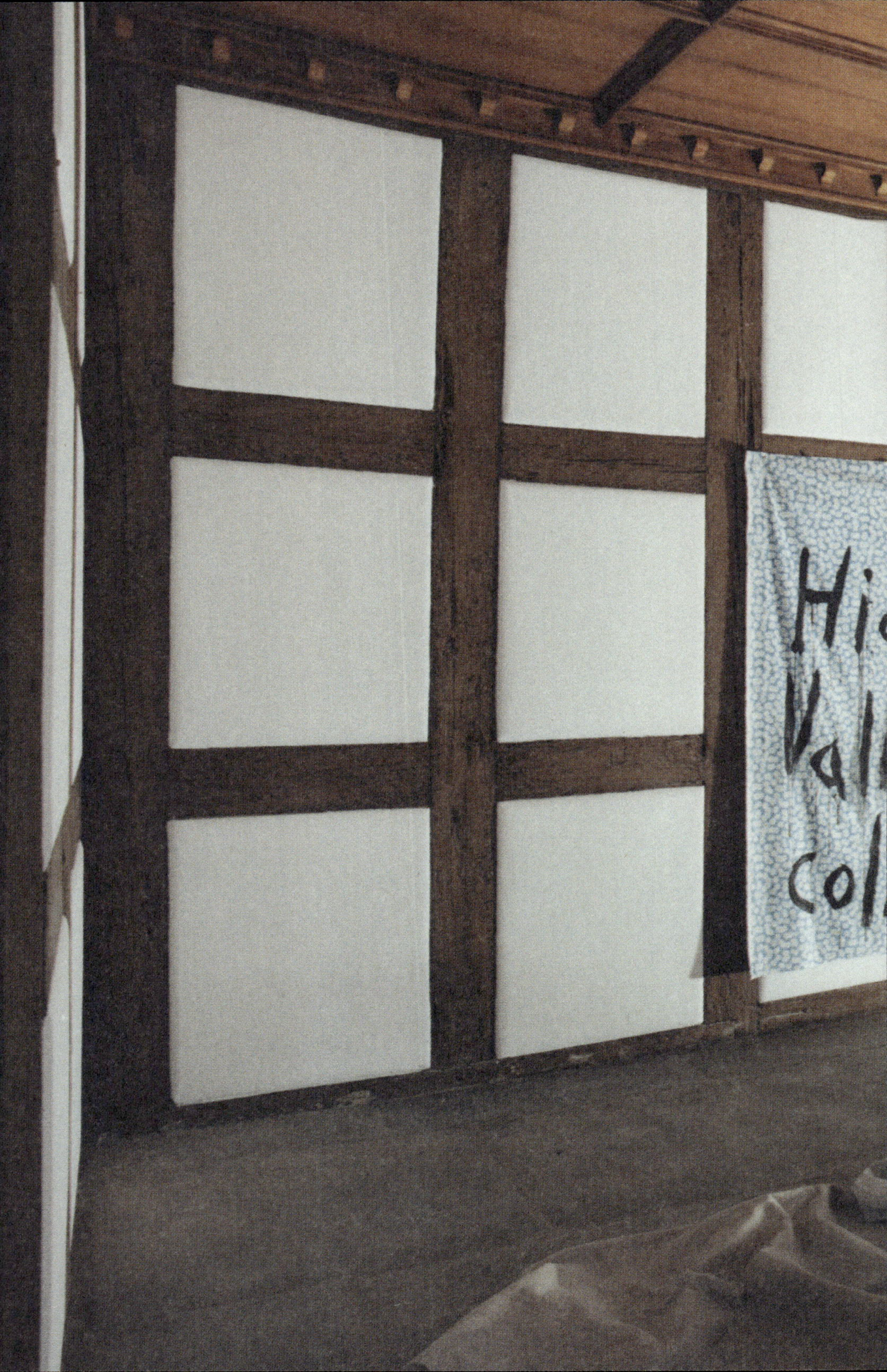

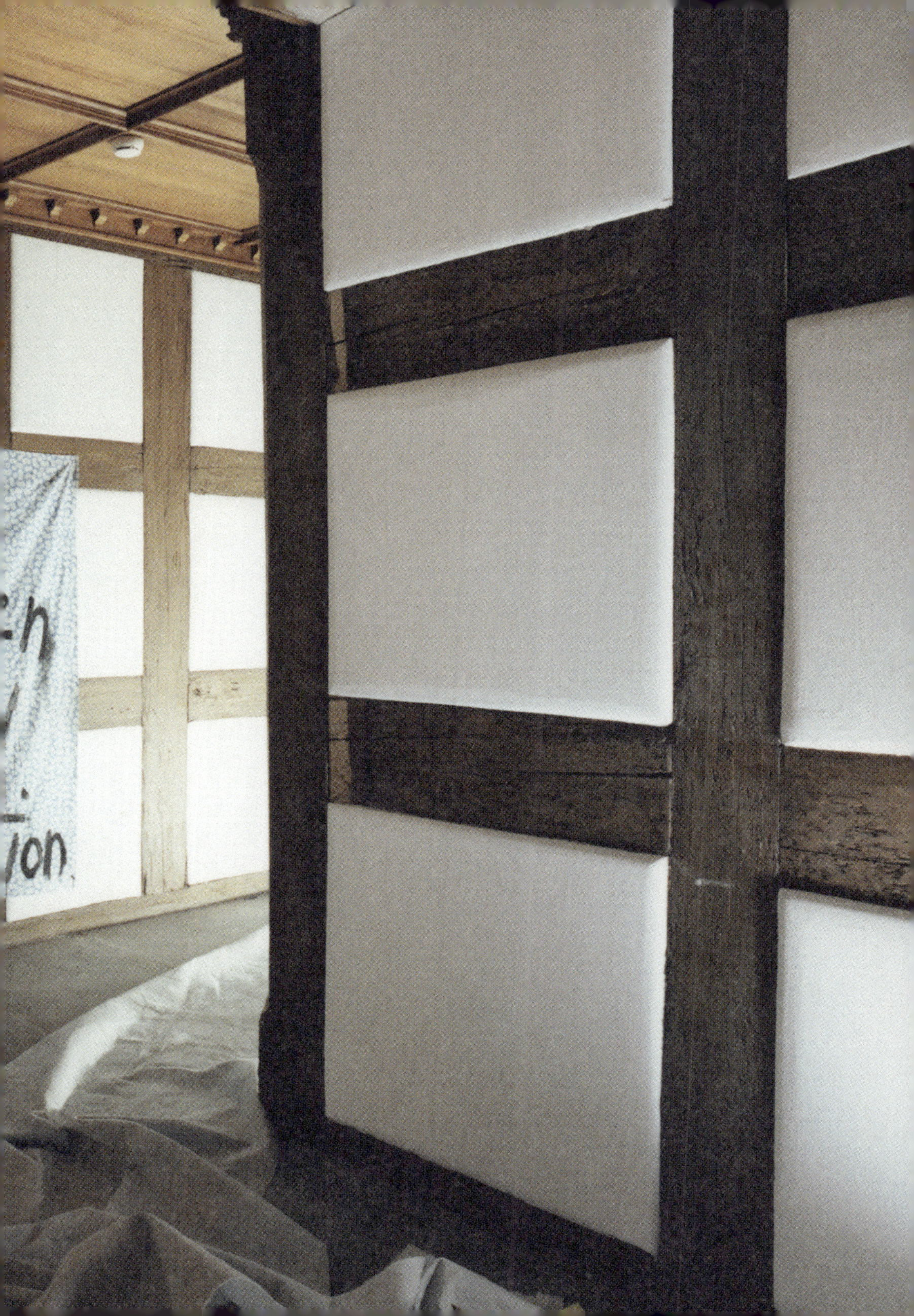

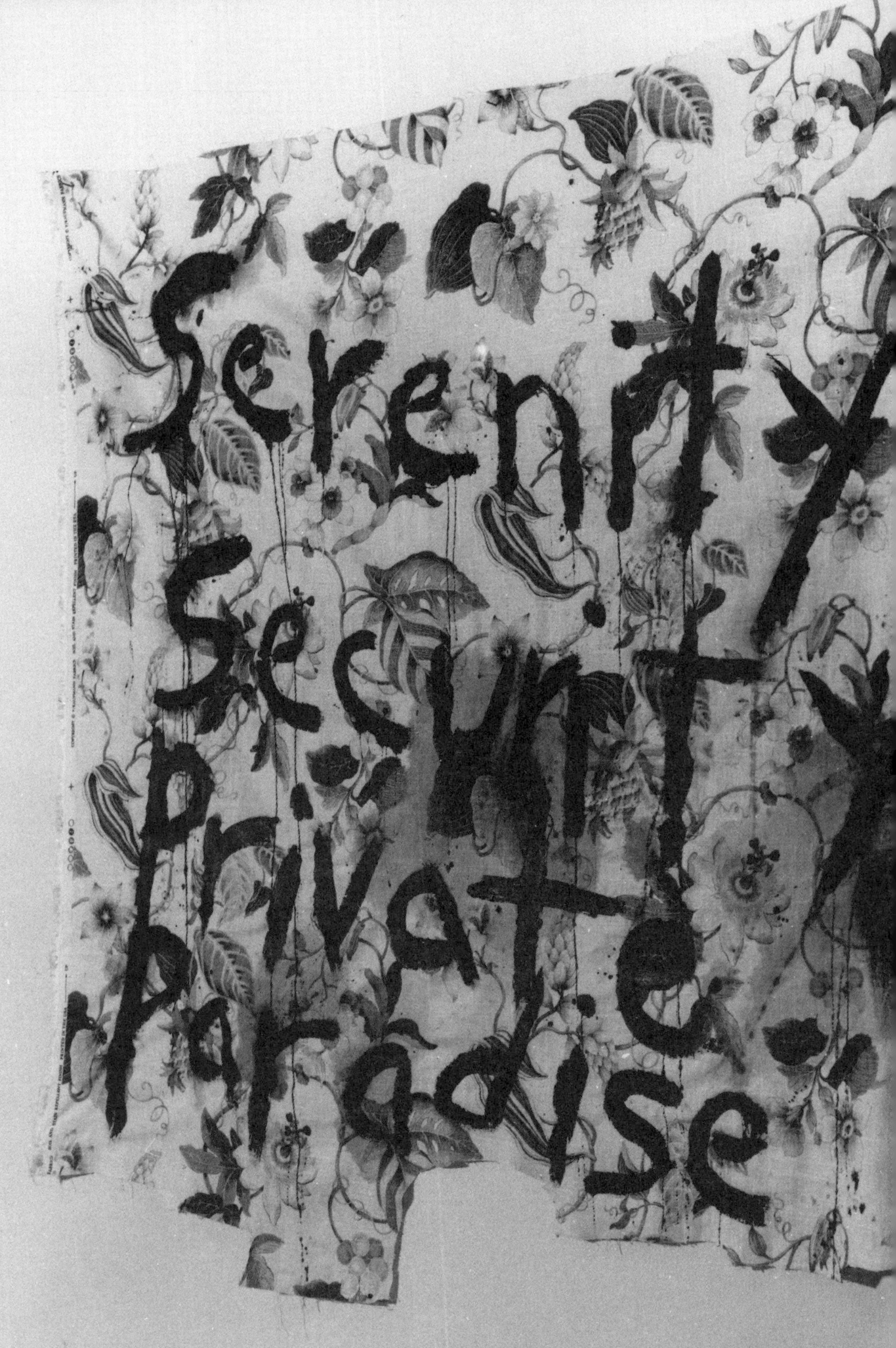
Serenity
Security
Private
Paradise

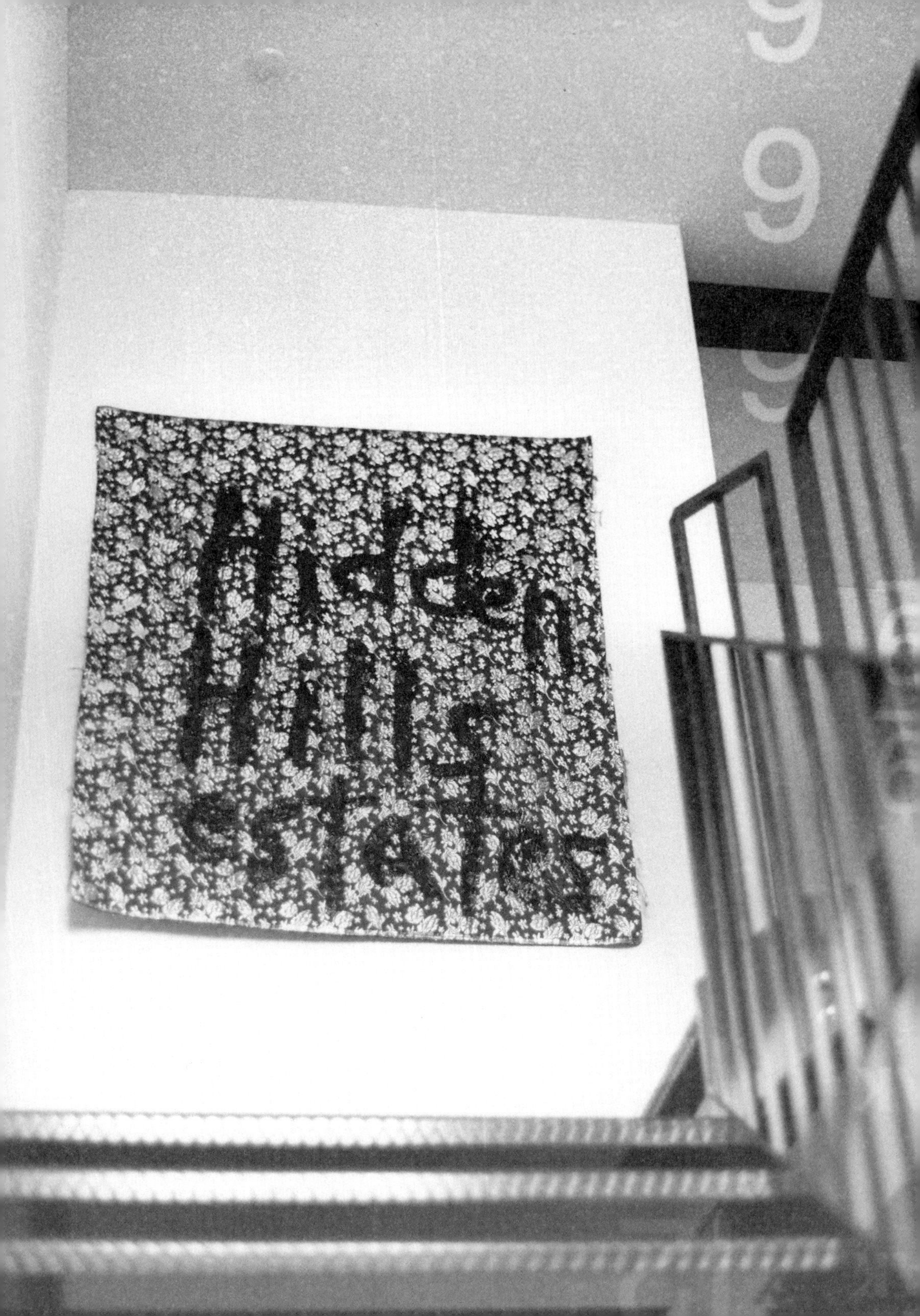
Hidden
Hills
estates

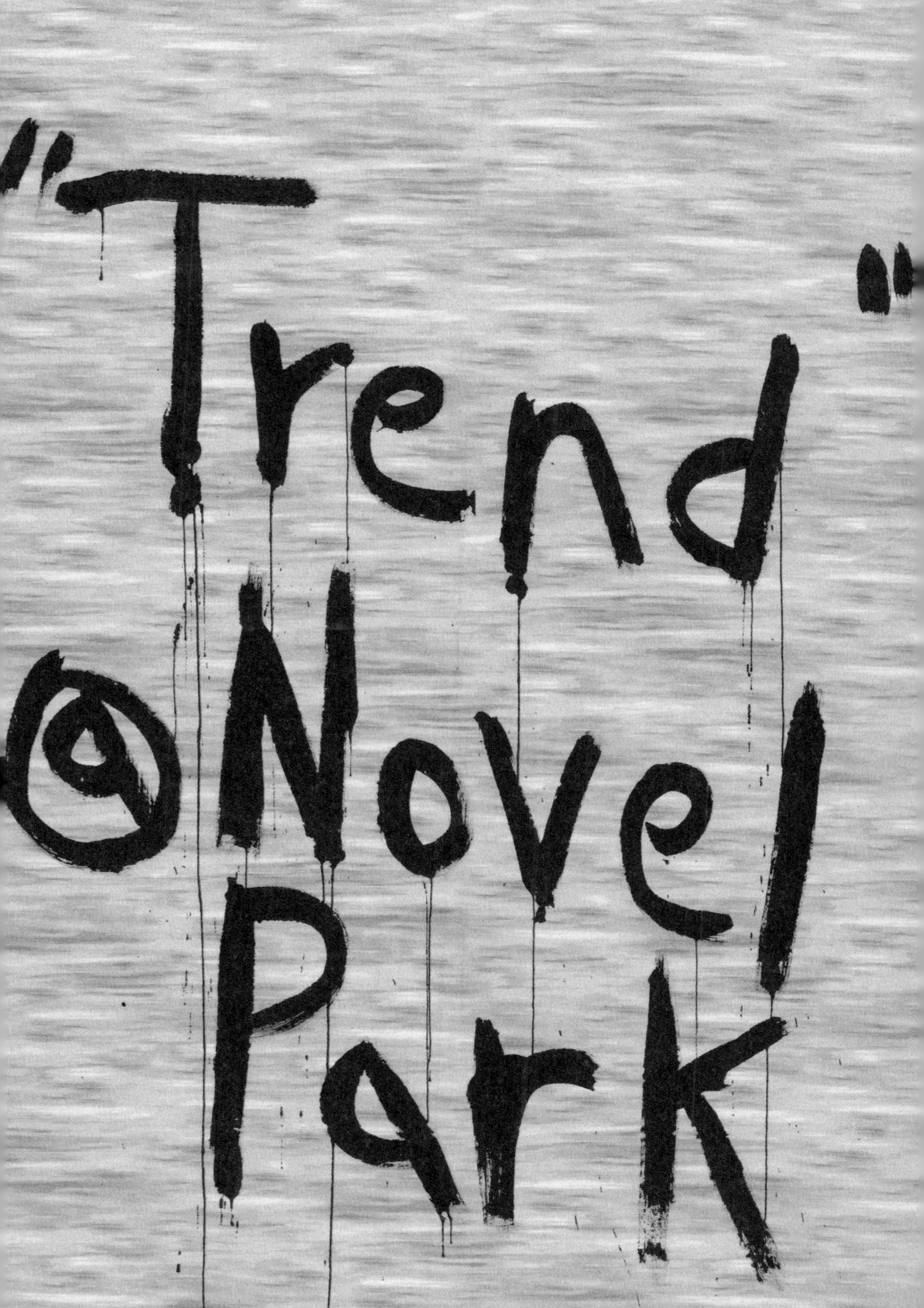
"Trend"
@Novel
Park

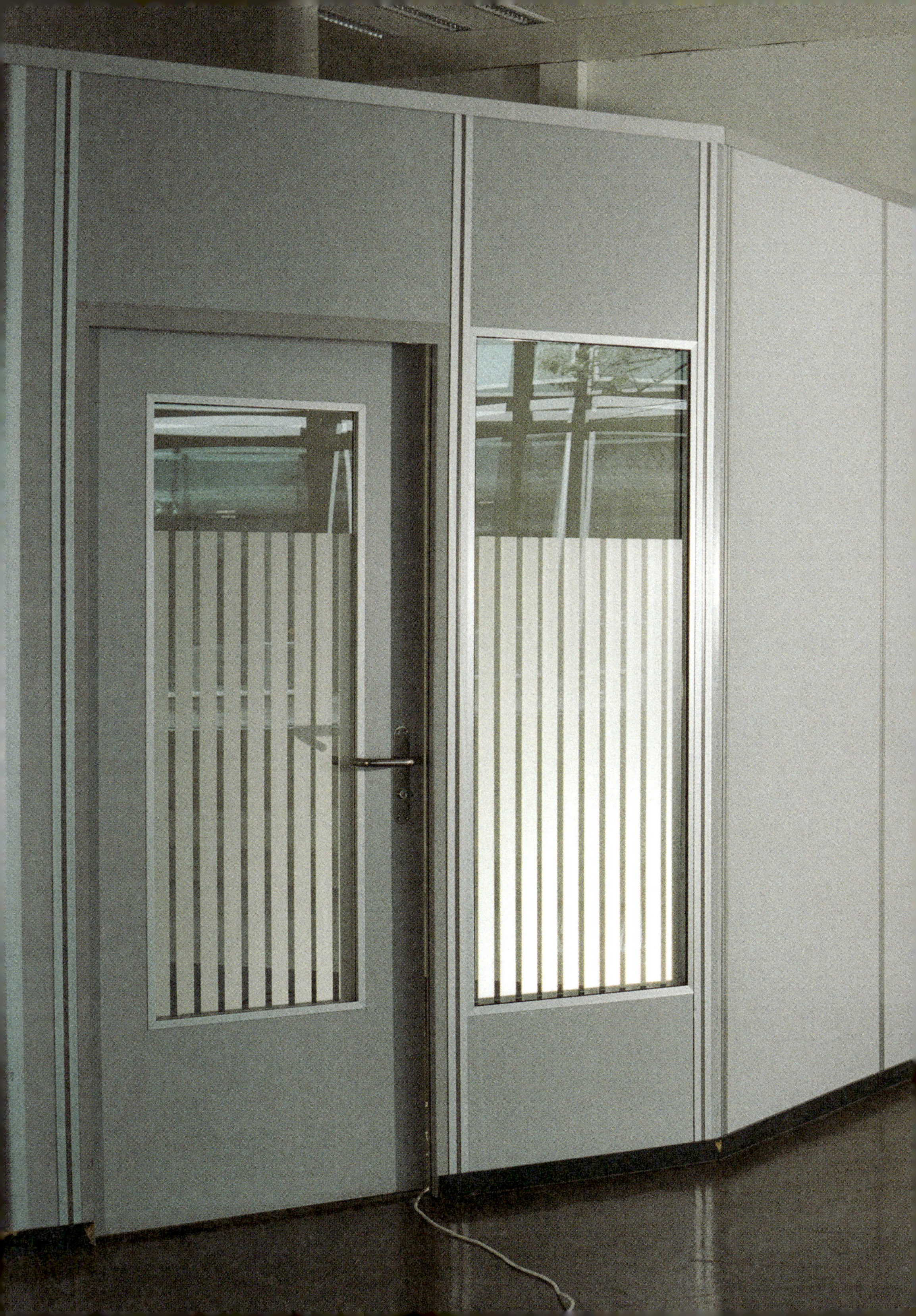

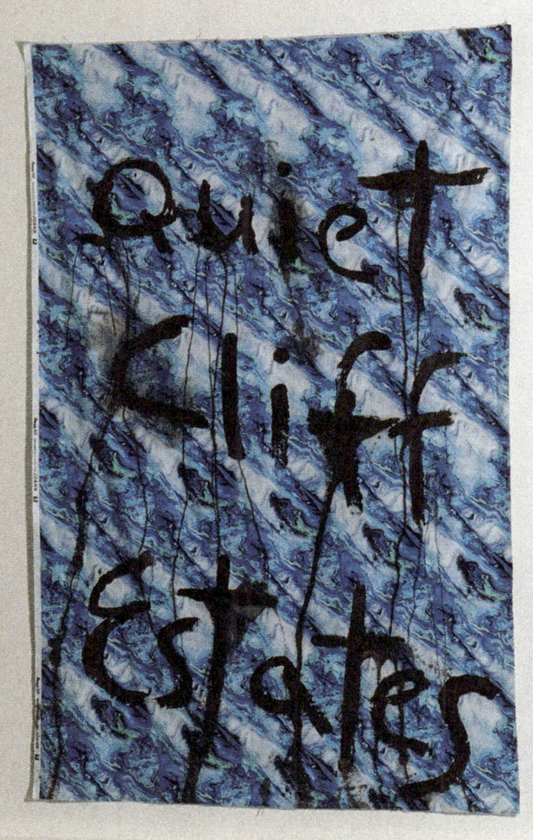
Quiet
Cliff
Estates

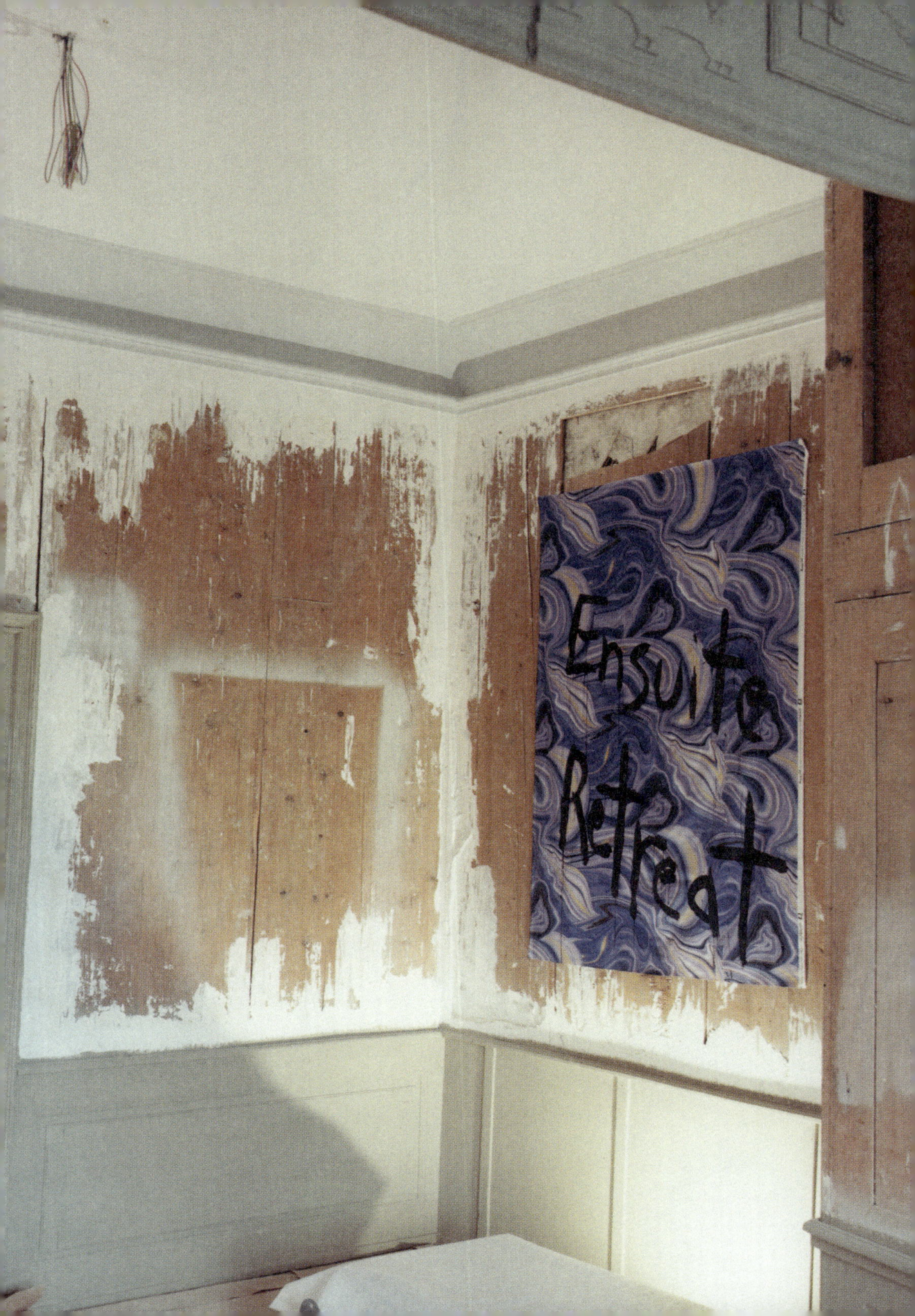
Ensuite
Retreat

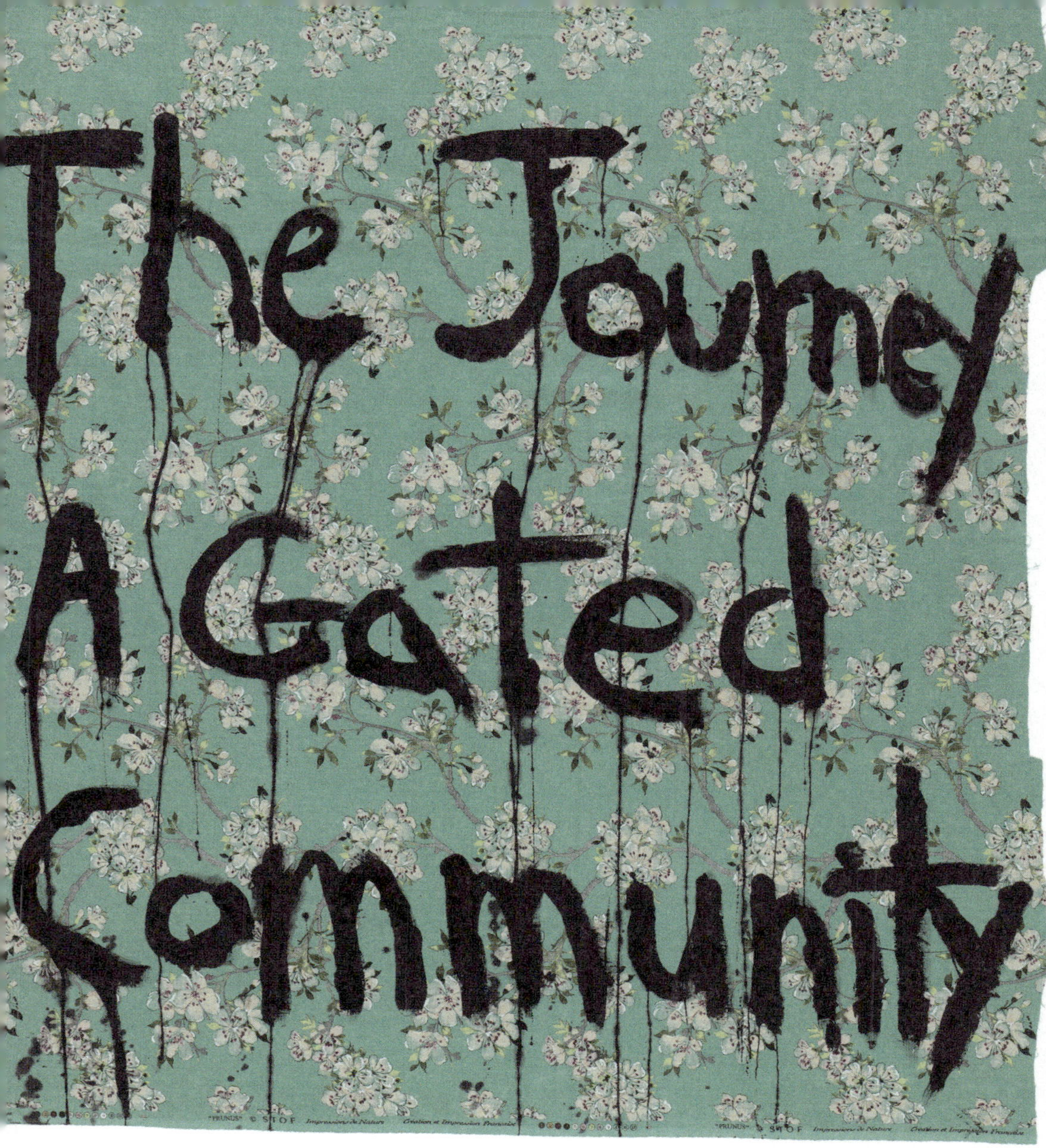

The Journey
A Gated
Community

"PRUNUS" © STOF Impressions de Nature Création et Impression Française
"PRUNUS" © STOF Impressions de Nature Création et Impression Française

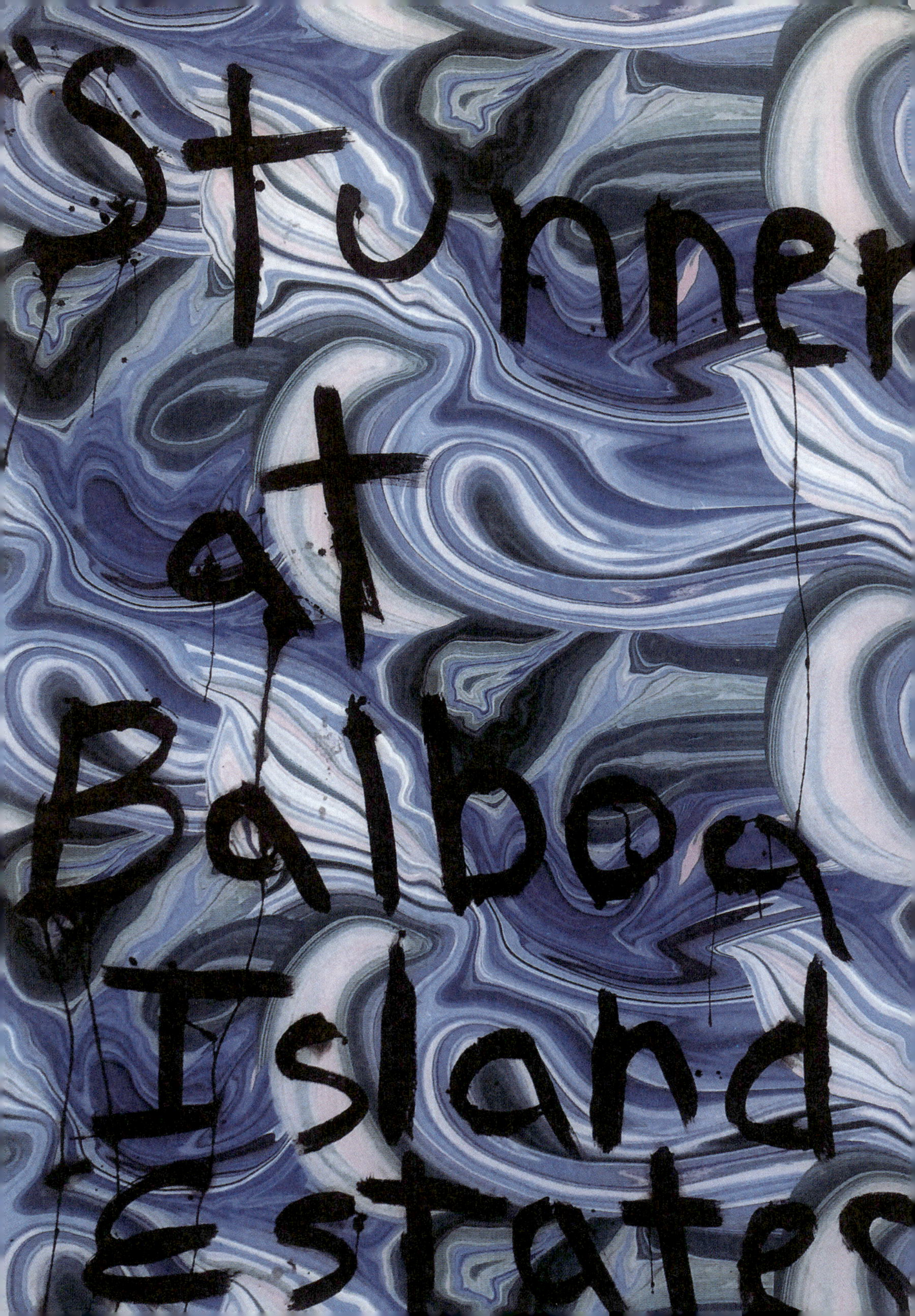
'Stunner
at
Balboa
Island
estates